4 FUMBLING FAIRY TALES

Lia London

Copyright © 2016 Lia London

All rights reserved.

ISBN: 10:1540325091
ISBN-13:978-1540325099

THE TALES

Princess Pennilopintha & the Magical Mouse
Page 5

Saccharine White & the 7 Dwarfs of SAGA
Page 23

The Quest for a Wide-Awake Princess
Page 38

Stormy Jane & the Damsel in Distress
Page 57

PRINCESS PENNILOPINTHA
& THE MAGICAL MOUSE

Once upon a time, there was a beautiful princess named Pennilopintha who lived in a stately castle in a peaceful kingdom.

Well, to be truthful, Princess Pennilopintha was rather plain. Granted, she had very nice, clear skin, but her nose was lumpy, and her hair was not a color of the sort that princes admire. It was neither shimmering gold nor raven black. It looked more like dust, and was just as prone to take flight in the slightest breeze.

But the castle *was* very stately. It was enormous, in fact, and even the most tenured servants occasionally got lost in its labyrinthine corridors.

And the kingdom was very peaceful indeed. This, however, was not due to any brilliant reigning philosophy constructed by her father, King Abnegolde, or any skill he had in creating a functional bicameral legislative body made up of representatives from the peasant farmers', blacksmiths', woodcutters' or millers' guilds. Rather, it had to do with the fact that the kingdom was so ridiculously far, far, *far* away from anything else that potential conquering (or at least pestering) forces couldn't be bothered to make the journey for such a small patch of land, no matter how fertile the fields or how full of magical mice. Especially because the obstacles in between said parcel of domain and the rest of the wide world of more accessible kingdoms included a forest full of man-eating spiky bindles, a terminally stormy lake with its very own serpent (*Not* a sea serpent. Salt dries out her scales.), and a vast desert infested with momphibraks of the worst disposition imaginable.

And this is why King Abnegolde, when he saw armored horses and banners cresting the hill into his valley, assumed that the approaching company must have been sent to seek out his daughter's hand in marriage. He hoped so. The sooner she was off his hands, the sooner he could *really* get on with his taxidermy hobby--something which made Pennilopintha terribly squeamish, so he tried not to practice it during supper.

Princess Pennilopintha, on the other hand,

sincerely hoped the approaching soldiers were merely lost. From her perch in the tallest tower (the obligatory room assignment for princesses in the mode), she could clearly see the flowing banners and recognized them from her World Kingdoms & Cultures class. The black flag carried the symbol of a ferocious boar's head. This, she wouldn't have minded so much, but the traditional swords that normally crossed behind such featured images as an embellishment were instead thrust graphically through the boar's head. The weavers had spared no effort in depicting the gore.

Down a few terraces, a line of buglers sounded an alarm, and King Abnegolde rode his mighty steed out to greet his guests. The Queen did not because, as is customary in these tales, she had died when Pennilopintha was just a baby. The King had not yet found a decent wicked stepmother to take her place.

"King Hognoggin! Is that you? It's been years!"

"Abnegolde, old man! How's that trick knee of yours? Still tricking you?" Here, the hairy visiting regent snorted, and Abnegolde guffawed. The various attendants gratefully hid their rolling eyes behind the visors of their helmets.

Flynnbrim, Hognoggin's chief valet, often daydreamed about a disastrous hunting trip that would allow Hognoggin's son, Prince Bumblesmutch, to ascend to the throne. True, the boy was dimwitted, but his capacity to craft lacy crullers and fountain fondues made the banquets more refined, and his incapacity to string more than three words together at a time made the meals much quieter. Altogether a more satisfactory sort of monarch.

Bumblesmutch, heeled like an obedient puppy, six paces behind his father as they entered the Great Dining Hall. He had not the acting skill to feign enthusiasm for the party, so he sat carefully and tried to hide his bulky frame from his father's view lest he should be called upon to speak.

"Aren't you going to eat your leg of goat?" said a small, acidic voice at his elbow.

He turned to find Princess Pennilopintha glaring at him.

"Don't like goat."

"Oh?" She eyed him skeptically.

"I like pastries."

"Oh?" She eyed him appreciatively.

He nodded heavily, already somewhat exhausted by the conversation.

"Allow me to show you our bakery while our fathers discuss their next hunt."

He nodded again, rising to his feet.

"It's a bit of a walk, and the maze of corridors can be confusing, but as long as you're at least as smart as a mouse..." Pennilopintha faltered as she saw beads of nervous sweat forming on Bumblesmutch's upper lip. "Here, hold my hand so we don't get lost."

And off they set. The two kings, scoffing and bubbling over their feast of roast quadrupeds and duck dumplings, saw this and winked knowingly at one another.

"There now, that's a good match!" said Abnegolde. "What say I give your boy my daughter's hand in marriage if you hunt up some momphibraks for me to stuff and mount on my walls?"

"As long as you give the rest of her, too!" Hognoggin roared with laughter, splattering wine in his glee.

"Take her! *Take* her!" King Abnegolde waved his hands. "And keep the momphibrak meat for sausage. It's very savory!"

"It's a deal!" grinned Hognoggin. "I'll even *savory* some for you!"

"You kill me, Hoggie!" chortled Abnegolde.

"I might one day!" he replied, wiping tears

of mirth from his eyes.

Further down the corridor, three turns to the left and one to the right, Bumblesmutch was about to break an all-time record by articulating a full-length sentence when he stopped short, rendered speechless by the splendor of the bakery.

"Do you *love* it? Daddy had it built for me so I wouldn't have to eat meat. I'm a vegetarian, you know, and I..." She fell silent, watching Bumblesmutch weep tears of wonder. Something in her heart melted when she saw his happiness.

Bumblesmutch muttered, "I stay here."

Pennilopintha folded her arms across her chest and regarded Bumblesmutch. "You know that by now my father has promised your father that you can marry me."

Bumblesmutch managed to close his mouth before it fell open again with surprise.

"And you realize that means I will have to go with you back to *your* father's kingdom."

The mournful look in Bumblesmutch's eyes as he gazed at the granite counters, brick ovens and large mixing basins confirmed her suspicion.

She tugged his sleeve gently and waved her

fingers in front of his face until she had his full attention. "You realize that this means we need to get rid of our fathers so that we both can stay *here* and live happily ever after?"

Bumblesmutch's left eyebrow quivered with concern.

"I'm not suggesting we kill them off!" assured the princess. "Just find a way for them to…go away."

Bumblesmutch stood straighter, as if filled with purpose. "Flynnbrim will help."

Flynnbrim was indeed eager to help under the condition that he would be assured a post under Princess Pennilopintha. Given that their natures were equally practical and peace-and-quiet-loving, she agreed. With a sudden air of authority, she said, "Come with me, gentlemen. It is time to cut the cheese."

Flynnbrim and Bumblesmutch exchanged a glance that showed they were nothing like the kings who would have snorted and giggled for half an hour. Trotting to catch up with Pennilopintha, they followed her through the maze of the castle corridors, up several flights of stairs and into a strangely cold and dark room in the west tower. Taking care to light the wall sconces from one of the candles in the hall candelabrum, Pennilopintha proudly pointed to a round table in the center of the room upon which stood a large yellowish mound of something pungent.

Flynnbrim's nostrils flared. "What *is* that?"

"Cheese, of course. Aged these two hundred years under the sole aid of a no-mold spell. We must carve a piece of it into some sort of recognizable shape and hope it pleases the Magical Mice. If it does, we get a wish." Pennilopintha moved to the table and picked up a knife. "I usually just make it into a star or something..."

"May I try?" asked Bumblesmutch.

Pennilopintha looked dubious, but Flynnbrim stepped forward and bowed graciously. "My lady, I believe His Majesty Prince Bumblesmutch may prove able to create a piece of cheese art that will please the Magical Mice."

With a shrug, Pennilopintha handed Bumblesmutch the knife and, while she and Flynnbrim carefully planned the wording of the wish, Bumblesmutch circled the cheese thoughtfully, chiseling a little here and poking a little there. By the time both were done—the wish wording took rather longer than it should have because Pennilopintha refused to include any hint of violence—everyone was quite pleased.

A low whistle at their feet heralded the entrance of a rotund white mouse that stood almost knee-high. "Now *that's* what I'm talking about! None of this cookie-cutter star or happy face slop. That—" he waved his forepaws appreciatively, "is a masterpiece."

Pennilopintha bowed respectfully. "High Wizard Skibble D'Spunk, we are so pleased to see you."

Skibble D'Spunk sniffed in response and leapt up onto the table to survey Bumblesmutch's creation. It looked like a mighty tree complete with leaves and birds' nests. On one of its lower branches perched a hissing, arch-backed kitten, terror literally etched in its face. Below it on the ground, made up of the pieces of cheese removed during carving, stood a sleek mouse with a crown. Its tail and fist were both held aloft in a clear threat to the kitten.

"It looks just like me." He turned back to the humans and nodded at Bumblesmutch. "Well, sir, you get to make the wish! What would you like?"

A panicked gurgle came from Pennilopintha, and Flynnbrim waved his entire body frantically to get Bumblesmutch's attention, but to no avail. Bumblesmutch shifted his feet nervously, cleared his throat and took a deep breath. "Is there any way feasible that you, High Wizard, could arrange for our fathers, the kings, to find it mutually beneficial and satisfactory to take up permanent residence back home in my father's kingdom, and allow me, the lovely Princess Pennilopintha, and Flynnbrim to remain here in this castle undisturbed from foreign or domestic affairs from now on and in perpetuity for our offspring, should we be so blessed?"

"Is that all?" squeaked Skibble D'Spunk amiably.

All three humans passed out for relief, shock or exhaustion as applicable. (The reader can surely discern which was which.)

When they all recovered an hour later, the mouse had eaten most of the cheese tree, though he left the terrified kitten and the commanding mouse untouched. Pounding a belch from his fuzzy white chest, he addressed them. "All better then?"

Bumblesmutch picked up the other two easily and placed them on either side of him.

"Good," said the mouse. "Now, since this wish requires Abnegolde to give up his kingdom, I'll just need one special thing from each of you—something you are willing to give up forever—to make this magic work. That's only fair, you know."

"I'd give up my throne to have this wish!" Pennilopintha clasped her hands over her mouth with a squeak, but it was clear from the mouse's expression that it was too late. "Oh, all right then." She shrugged. "I'll sit in a recliner."

Bumblesmutch spoke with his usual labored effort. "Take whipped cream."

Flynnbrim, startled, turned to the Prince. "Are you quite sure, Your Majesty? The pastries--"

Bumblesmutch grinned. "Use ice cream."

"Ah, clever, sir. Very clever."

"And you?" The High Wizard twirled his tail idly and glared at the valet.

"I ... don't really own much," said Flynnbrim evasively.

"Your fur coat?" suggested Bumblesmutch.

"Ew!" shrieked Pennilopintha.

"My fur coat!" complained Flynnbrim, and he, too, covered his mouth with both hands, also too late to retract.

"Perfect!" declared Skibble D'Spunk. "Couldn't have made better choices myself. This'll be a snap! Let's get those things out to the courtyard. C'mon. Don't drag your tails!"

In the courtyard, Bumblesmutch set down Pennilopintha's throne (she had carried his giant bowl of whipped cream down from the kitchen after watching in astonishment how swiftly he worked the dairy into a lather). The prince turned to look at the High Wizard Skibble D'Spunk and Flynnbrim. "Is this good?" He dusted invisible specks from the golden armrests.

"Very good." Skibble D'Spunk scratched his chin in a very un-catlike way. "You drape the fur coat over the front so it covers the whole thing," he added, gesturing to the reluctant Flynnbrim.

The valet obliged, thin-lipped in his flourish, after pausing to check for loose change in the pockets.

"Um. Where do you want this?" Pennilopintha hefted the bowl.

The mouse studied the heaping swirl of froth carefully. "Have you got a spoon?"

Bumblesmutch drew a wooden spoon from what heretofore would have been mistaken for the sheath of a mid-sized saber.

Skibble D'Spunk took it without letting his eyes drift from the bowl of whipped cream. Then, wielding the wooden spoon like a broadsword, he became a blur of white fur and cream. When at last he finished, even Bumblesmutch stood in awe.

"You aren't the only one who got A's in the Decorative Culinary Arts," smirked the mouse.

"It's a queen!" gasped Bumblesmutch.

The High Wizard nodded respectfully in Pennilopintha's direction. "She will be your benevolent stepmother, if your father isn't too stupid to take the bait." He snapped into a rigid stance, raised his arms and commanded: "All of you close your eyes and think of something that makes you very happy. Then, when I count to three, speak its name and open your eyes again to behold happily-ever-magic beyond compare. One, two—no peeking now--three!"

"Hot cherry tarts!"

"Jasmine bubble baths!"

"Green bean smoothies!"

The humans opened their eyes and collectively gasped enough air to inflate a large weather balloon. There before them stood a golden legged, thick-furred momphibrak, and standing beside it, ready to mount the noble beast, was the fairest (albeit palest) queen imaginable.

"Hello, my dear Pennilopintha," she said in an airy voice. "You look like you need some alone time with your charming suitor. I was thinking I might lure that handsome father of yours back to Hognoggin's castle. Do you think he'd be inclined to join me? Then you could get to that bubble bath."

"That wasn't actually me," stammered the princess.

Flynnbrim cleared his throat and began humming a tuneless melody that would later be adopted by a game show host to be used during the most grueling round of trivia questions.

The queen noticed this and blushed a faint shade of eggshell before returning her gaze to Pennilopintha. "What do you think, dear? Would he like that?"

"*Would* I?" blustered Abnegolde, who had just appeared in his finery to welcome this latest guest. "Hey, Hognoggin!" he bellowed over his shoulder. "Get a load of this vision I'm having."

Hognoggin sauntered out with a well-roasted leg of something stout in one fist and a goblet of something fruity in the other. He took one look at the assembly and dunked the drumstick into the wine. Tossing both carelessly over the wall, he wiped his hands on his leggings and approached the momphibrak with cautious wonder.

"Why does it not hiss and spit and kick?" he whispered.

"It is a magical momphibrak," announced Skibble D'Spunk grandly. He had gone unnoticed too long for his taste, and made a great show of placing himself in the kings' line of sight. Both men seemed to take a moment to focus on this abnormally large rodent, and Abnegolde stifled a girlish scream. As if to confirm the mouse's claim, however, the white queen leapt gracefully onto the back of the golden-legged momphibrak, stroking its fur gently and slipping her dainty white riding boots into the deep pockets on the beast's side that acted as built-in stirrups. A moment later, she and the momphibrak had pranced out of the courtyard and were making haste towards the horizon.

In a burst of motion, the two kings quickly found their own mighty steeds and mounted them without waiting for a hunting party. They galloped after the white queen on her momphibrak at top speed. "I get the beauty, and you get the beast, right-o?" called Abnegolde as he bounced along.

"Fine by me," agreed Hognoggin. "She looks a bit pale to me. Besides, I've got my own raven-haired bride at home. Can't wait to catch that strange momphibrak, though, and skin it to make a fur coat! And what about those golden legs?"

But Abnegolde cared not a whit for the momphibrak. He stared dreamily after the creamily clad woman whose riding skills far exceeded his own and vowed to himself he would woo her to wife if he had to follow her through the desert, around the stormy lake and into the heart of the forest laden with man-eating spiky bindles. He would even give up being king.

Which is exactly what he ended up doing.

Fortunately, the magical momphibrak acted as a magnet of sorts for all the other momphibraks, whose tempers it appeased with a flick of its golden armrest hoof. The happily grunting momphibraks made such a ruckus as they reached the shores of the lake that the serpent dared not show her head, and the procession stampeded gleefully around the banks, skirting the worst of the rain clouds. From there, they all plunged deep into the woods, tearing such a path in their wake that the spiky bindles decided to back off the man-eating for a day and try mushroom soup.

It wasn't until Hognoggin's own castle came into view at the base of a wide valley that the momphibraks dispersed and began grazing like throne-shaped cattle. At this point, the pace of the white queen's momphibrak slowed to a leisurely amble, and she alighted on a rock to await the kings, letting the magical creature wander off into the valley.

When the kings came abreast of her, Hognoggin winked slyly. "Why don't you two hurry on to the castle? I'm sure my bride, Glorisplenda will receive you gladly. I'm going to go pick up a little something for dinner," he grinned, surveying the miles of green farmland now dotted with docile momphibraks. He clicked his tongue at his steed and set off after the golden-legged momphibrak.

Abnegolde blushed down to his boots and back up to his collar again before finally extending his hand to the white queen. "May I take you the rest of the way to Hognoggin's castle?"

"Why thank you." Her fingers felt as soft as coconut oil in his hand, and her breath smelled lite, yet sweetened.

"Do you have a name, fair queen?"

"Why don't you know? It's Hapleigh Evveraft!"

Back in Abnegolde's kingdom—now

Flynnbrim's kingdom, Pennilopintha and Bumblesmutch stayed on at the castle, married, and began their own Vegetarian Bakery and Culinary Cafe which operated out of the west wing. Its white mouse shaped placard was inscribed with the popular slogan, "No animals were harmed in the making of this mousse!"

King Flynnbrim recovered from the loss of his fur coat and learned to live peacefully and fashionably once he'd married the local tailor's daughter, and they all lived excessively happily ever after as per Bumblesmutch's well-worded wish.

SACCHARINE WHITE & THE 7 DWARFS OF SAGA

Once upon a time, there was a princess who had hair as black as night, lips as red as blood, and skin as white as snow, so naturally, everyone who saw her freaked out.

Her ghostly appearance created such an uproar that she often found it easier to retreat into the woods amongst the man-eating spiky bindles who were not as skittish.

One day, while gathering mushrooms and thistles (she was not the "flowers and berries" sort of princess), she happened upon a charmingly squat little cottage. Peering in through the open window, she marveled to see that all the furniture inside was very small. She counted seven little wooden chairs around a long, cluttered table. Up against the far wall, she saw a rocking chair, a broom, a mop and a basket full of moth-eaten socks.

Oh no! she thought. *I'm not falling into this kind of trap. I'm not doing anyone's cleaning or mending. I'm a proper princess!* She turned to run, only to stumble over a row of neatly dressed dwarfs in fashionable suits and patent leather penny loafers. They all had abnormally good hair and capped teeth.

Immediately she knew she was in the worst danger of her life.

"Hey!" cried one of the dwarfs excitedly. "I know you. You're Glorisplenda's little sister." He snapped his fingers and chewed his lip, trying to recall the name.

"Saccharine White!" offered another dwarf with cosmetically enhanced dimples.

"Ooooh!" the others said greedily. "The *unwanted* princess!"

Saccharine stood with her hands on her hips seriously calculating how many dwarfs she could knock over with one good swipe of her mushroom basket. "Yeah. Thanks for that, gentlemen. Always good to know I've kept my celebrity status. Now, if you'll excuse me—"

"Oh, you have! We *love* stories like yours!" said the first dwarf winningly. His name was Charmy. The dimpled one was Smarmy. Two of the others were called Looney and Twit, and the remaining three were so like each other that no one could tell them apart.

Poor Saccharine had fallen amongst the seven dwarfs of SAGA (the Scandal and

Gossip Association), infamous for trumpeting all the dirtiest royal secrets they could discover and generally creating celebrity unrest in otherwise peaceful domains far and near. (This is why they fit in so well with the man-eating spiky bindles, by the way.)

Saccharine eyed the path she'd taken through the woods and wondered what a high-speed chase through the poison ivy would do to her. Was it worth another bath in calamine lotion to get away from the paparazzi?

Saccharine chewed her lip some more, eventually peeling a layer of chapped skin and drawing blood. Irritated, she wiped her lip with the back of her hand, but not before one of the dwarfs (the one named Twit), gasped in horror. "Is she...a vampire?!"

"*Ooooh!* Vampires are all the rage right now!" squealed Smarmy, rubbing his hands.

"No, now it's all about zombies," corrected Looney.

Charmy jumped in. "Come, Miss White. Won't you join us for an interview?"

"I'd love to chat, but I still have to—*Oh my goodness!* Are those *cotton* socks I see?" This had the desired effect of confusing the dwarfs, and Saccharine continued carefully, "Because, if they are, I've heard those are worth a barrel of gold nowadays."

"What?"

"Huh?"

Saccharine smiled with artificial sweetness. "Don't you know? All the recently domesticated momphibraks have been breaking into the cotton fields and eating the crops. The farmers are at a total loss. Cotton prices are up, up, up!"

"They are?" Twit turned slowly towards the door of the cottage.

"Indeed! I know a weaver in my brother-in-law's kingdom that buys used cotton socks, refurbishes them, and sells them to the gentry. Why don't you bring me your socks to wash, and I'll go get some kindling for a fire. I'll boil them clean in a big pot."

The three almost identical dwarfs narrowed their eyes. "What's in it for you?"

"Oh, the weaver gives me a kickback if I find quality cotton. Hurry now!"

There was a beat of silence before each of the dwarfs dashed into the cottage, eager to be the first to bring his socks to be washed by the celebrity goth vampire princess. While they tumbled over each other in their haste, Saccharine slipped out of the clearing and tore through the poison ivy as fast as her feet could carry her.

Saccharine's industrial strength support hose and long skirts protected her legs from the poison ivy as she ran, but when she slipped on a fresh hair ball left by a spiky bindle, she landed flat on her back. With the wind knocked out of her, she couldn't move in time to save her arms.

Itchity scratch itchy scratchy itchy scratch--

"Aha! There you are!" beamed Charmy. "Did you have a little mishap?"

Itchity scratchity itch itch scratch...

"Just a little one." She raked her fingernails over her pasty white skin.

"Oh, how unfortunate." Charmy clucked his tongue in the least maternal way imaginable. "Here, let me help you. We've brought the cauldron for boiling the water."

Saccharine White allowed the dwarfs to heave her to her feet and lead her through the underbrush to a stream. She noted, with reluctant admiration, that their suits were spun from finely twined wiggledy silk, known to repel all noxious oils from plants and hair products.

Itchy itchy scratch scratch.

"Would you like to use our laundry soap, or yours?" asked a soft voice.

Saccharine turned to scan the faces of the dwarfs and realized that the voice came from one of the three nearly identical ones. Her brow wrinkled with suspicion. "Yours?"

"Are you sure?" She couldn't tell which dwarf spoke because their lips didn't move. They just held fast in pleasantly patronizing grins.

Scratch scratch scratchity SCRATCH!

"Well, given that I didn't anticipate washing socks during this particular jaunt into the forest—"

"Splendid!" said Smarmy. "Our recipe helps with the poison ivy residue, too."

"Gimme!" barked Saccharine, snatching the small box of powder from the dwarf and sprinkling it onto her arms.

Then she built a fire, kindling it with underbrush and igniting it with a gilded flint rock. As the water bubbled, Saccharine observed them observing her and tried not to shudder at the infrequency of their blinks. At last she dumped the cotton socks into the hot water and plunged her arms in afterwards. The soap powder sifted off her arms and into the water, and she began to scrub. The water actually soothed her itchy scratchy arms, and she found her mood softening. She didn't even flinch when the dwarfs circled around her—ever so casually pulling out their parchments and quills—and began to ask seemingly benign questions about her favorite latte flavors, her relaxation techniques, her dressmaker's quirks, and any secret vendettas she had against her sister Glorisplenda.

About the time the last of the bubbles popped, Saccharine hung the final white cotton sock on a nearby branch to dry. She realized too late what she had divulged and what had to be done to stop any ensuing scandal. She turned and smiled sweetly—which frightened the dwarfs immensely—and asked if she might sing them a song while the socks dried. Before they could answer, she belted forth in a dulcet baritone voice, "I'm wishing for the one I hate to lose me today..." The woodland ravens and spiky bindles gathered to caw and shriek in harmony, and soon the SAGA dwarfs drifted off into nightmare-ridden sleep.

Now she had to make her move—once and for all—to rid the land of the gossipmongers and ensure a little well-deserved privacy for all nonconformist royals everywhere.

Saccharine looked about for something on which to dry her hands, but found nothing. With a smirk, she eyed the coattails of wiggledy silk. "Might as well ruin their suits before they try to ruin my life," she muttered. She knelt down and rubbed her hands on

Twit's sleeve carefully. "Hm, that's nice stuff." Gingerly picking up the edge of his lapel, she ran her fingers along the silk.

Twit snuffled in his sleep, moaning sadly. "Missed my calling... Wanted to run a hair salon..."

Saccharine jolted with surprise, and then realized he was only talking in his sleep. She crouched near the three nameless dwarfs and listened. "Why can't they ever remember my name?" whined one of them softly. "If I could just break off and go solo with my lute picking act..."

Saccharine crawled to the next dwarf. "...used to be best archer...now just shooting pictures..."

His triplet scowled in his sleep. "Why can't I just count the money? Must I work for it, too?"

Silently, she stood up and watched the circle of dwarfs sleep. Looney was humming a daffy tune in between loud snores, and Smarmy seemed to be practicing his grin. Charmy, however, was quite agitated. "Not the hair!" he squeaked. "Don't touch the hair!"

Saccharine chuckled to herself and glanced down at her hands. They had a pinkish flush from all of the scrubbing—or was it the laundry soap? Stooping as close to Smarmy as she dared, she checked her reflection in his teeth. Black hair, red lips...but was that *flesh-*colored flesh?

"I'll have to chance it." She resumed her song for a few minutes, being careful to linger closely to each dwarf's ear in turn. They fell all the more deeply into their dreams, and at last, she winked to the spiky bindles. "No snacking on them now," she whispered. "I have a better idea!"

She turned and ran through the forest, this time avoiding the poison ivy paths, and eventually arrived at her father's castle. The guards did not recognize her, but nor did they stop her. She looked quite lovely for once, flushed from the run (or was it the soap?).

"Daddy? Oh, Daddy? I think I've found you a new Treasurer, a couple of court minstrels, a royal barber and an archer for your army!"

Her father looked up from his newsparchments and stared. "Why, Saccharine, my little girl! When did you grow up and start taking your job as Director of Human Resources seriously? I thought you hated people!"

"Um. I'm not going to answer that right now. Can I borrow your hunting horse? I need to pack the dwarfs out of the forest."

Her father, returning to his news, waved her away. "I never understand a word kids say nowadays..."

Back in the woods, Saccharine hefted all the sleeping dwarfs except Charmy and Smarmy onto the annoyed horse and used the clean socks to lash them together so they wouldn't fall off. As they ambled back home, the dwarfs gradually roused themselves from her song-enchanted sleep feeling refreshed despite being mostly upside-down.

"Oh good! You're up," said Saccharine cheerily.

"Who are you?" asked Twit groggily.

"It's me, Saccharine White, and I've got great news for you." She explained the staff vacancies at her father's castle, and each of them sat up with wide eyes.

"What's the catch?" asked the triplet dwarfs in unison.

"Three things. First, you don't write about what you see at the castle. Just live with us in peace and quiet."

"I'm fine with that!" declared Twit.

"It's Charmy and Smarmy that love the spotlight of the scandal business," said Looney.

"Yes, and that leads me to the second condition. You help me teach Charmy and Smarmy a lesson."

The three nameless dwarfs rumbled with delight. "Oh! We've been planning this for years. Just wait 'til you hear what we've got in store for them! What's the third condition?"

"I want the recipe for your laundry soap."

Once the dwarfs had been deposited in front of Saccharine's father for their official post approvals, she hurried back (as per their plan) and hoisted Charmy and Smarmy onto the horse, singing to them all the way, so they'd remain in slumber. In the courtyard, she whistled for the dwarfs, who all pranced out in their new professional attire, beaming with joy.

Twit stepped forward, brazenly flourishing a long razor, as though it were a battle sword. The others kept their distance, fearing blood splatters on their fine new uniforms, but Twit's hand was sure. Poised for the kill above Charmy, he began slicing and dicing away at the gossiping ring leader's hair. (This was no small feat, for it had been fortified by at least three illegal chemicals.) When he finished, he bowed before the applause. Charmy's hair now looked exactly like the hide of a spiky bindle after a particularly vicious windstorm.

Saccharine motioned for them to be quiet, and began humming softly while Twit turned his attention to Smarmy. With delicate care, he removed every last wisp of facial hair, including the eyebrows, and then pinned Smarmy's top lip open using a hair clip. Thoughtfully and gently, he used Saccharine's red lipstick (which he also forbade her ever to use again) to draw tiny murals of dancing cherubs on each of Smarmy's white, capped teeth. The end result was breathtakingly hideous.

The other dwarfs now moved in with stealth, lifting Charmy and Smarmy into the fountain where they propped them in embarrassing poses.

Now came the hard part. Saccharine had to sing non-stop until the court painter had completed a four-by-eight-foot masterpiece of the spectacle. It took two weeks; Saccharine's voice was raw, and her eyes were blood-shot, but it was worth it.

When the work was completed, she flopped forward into the fountain with a splash (she had neither bathed nor slept in all that time), and the sudden silence jolted Charmy and Smarmy awake.

Charmy tried to run his fingers through his hair and gasped.

Smarmy tried to close his mouth because his teeth felt fuzzy and dry, but he couldn't.

"Wha haffening here?" he demanded, fumbling with the lip clip.

Twit, Looney, and the three other dwarfs (who, incidentally, were named John, David and Steve) snickered and pointed to the portrait.

Charmy took one look at the monstrosity and screamed. Smarmy whimpered. Saccharine roused herself and grinned cunningly.

"Now that we have your attention," she said with the same tone Charmy had used so many times before announcing the secrets of the local royalty, "may I presume you would like to strike a mutually beneficial contract?"

"B-b-blackmail?" cried Charmy.

"Tsk, tsk, what a foul word. Nothing of the sort. We'd like to offer you an opportunity." She gestured to the five rehabilitated dwarfs. "These fine gentlemen have all found lucrative and fulfilling positions in our castle and kingdom, and we would like to offer you the same."

"I won't dig latrines," sniffed Smarmy.

"No, you won't be dealing in muck

anymore," assured Saccharine ironically. "You will be the royal family's chief publicists, with the charge of making us look Brilliant, Witty and Just at every opportunity. For this you will be paid handsomely. Any failure to do so, however, would result in the unfortunate kingdom-wide tour of this piece of art—with you gentlemen following behind in a live re-enactment."

"Oh, that won't be necessary!" Charmy leaped out of the fountain, struggling to muster his suavity. "Our every aim would be to please the royal persons."

Smarmy, rubbing his lip and wiping his tears, simply nodded.

"Well then, this will all end very happily, indeed!" said Saccharine.

And it did.

Surprisingly so.

The kingdom responded so favorably to the positive light in which their regents were now portrayed that they became more productive workers, singing merrily (and not at all dream-inducingly) as they labored. Charmy and Smarmy even managed to get side gigs talking up the more prominent businessmen, inserting subliminal advertisements for jelly tarts, wiggledy silk stockings, and broccoli into their weekly shows. For these efforts, they became rich beyond their fondest hopes and moved forever out of the forest of the spiky bindles. Their cottage was soon taken over by a small family of bears who were very fond of hot cereal and long walks.

Saccharine took long bubble baths in laundry soap and dabbled with softer shades of pink lipstick. It wasn't long before people praised her beauty above that of Glorisplenda, and she had no shortage of eligible suitors for her hand in marriage. But that's another story...

THE QUEST FOR A WIDE-AWAKE PRINCESS

Prince Jack had not been given a good name (otherwise he would have been called something like Bumblesmutch, Evergard, or Floyd), but he was taught the value of hard work, which was surprising given that such knowledge was generally considered inappropriate for princes in the mode. Thus, when it came time for him to choose a bride, which is always in that nebulous age range between eighteen and decaying-father's-pending-death, Prince Jack found himself watching the red carpet runway with an eye for some spunk. He knew how to pick a winning racehorse. She would be lean, sleek, prancing with barely contained energy, holding her head high. Unfortunately, the princesses parading before him who exhibited such characteristics tended to trip over their gowns and/or passing courtiers. The resulting pile of squealing invalids pleased the court physician, but left poor Prince Jack wanting someone a bit sturdier.

So, he mounted his own steed, a freshly retired racehorse named Trifecta Trumper (Trump for short), and set out in search of princesses from kingdoms far farther away. He guessed that the "Eligible Prince" memo had been lost in royal spam boxes due to the mass emailing his father had sent out, so he thought he'd let people know in person. Jack's mother (who obviously had a name, but no one knew it because she was just "the queen" and "Her Majesty) kissed him farewell, wished him luck, and tucked a spare mane-toupee in his saddlebag for Trump, who was very vain for a horse.

Jack rode in and out of days—which was a navigational nightmare, owing to Trump's penchant for left-hand turns—until he reached a quiet but expansive castle with impressively manicured shrubberies. "Someone here works hard. Hopefully that reflects the noble work ethic of the reigning monarchs and any feminine offspring of marriageable age who might live and rule here."

Trump shook his mane and began chewing a hole in a frighteningly spherical rhododendron bush.

Jack jerked the reins. "Trump, I'll never

make a good impression if you eat their ornamental plants. Let's go." They galloped across the drawbridge, which he noted was merely for decoration since the moat consisted of a shallow trench filled with assorted perennials in pink and gold. "Not fearsome, but efficient," he observed.

Trump snorted in agreement and came to an abrupt halt, pitching Jack headlong into the great wooden doors of the castle.

Jack managed to remain conscious, but glared at Trump. "That wasn't funny. How can I make a good impression with a giant lump on my forehead?"

At that very moment, the door swung inward to reveal an abnormally lanky butler. "I beg your pardon?" He frowned down at Jack who had not yet regained his feet. "Did you knock, sir?"

Standing, Jack rubbed the bump on his head. "In a manner of speaking, yes." He puffed his chest out and took on his most princely stance. "I am Prince Jack. I have traveled far and wide in search of—"

"Up two flights, fourth door on the right." The butler heaved the door wider. "You may park the horse around back, or I can call someone to do it for you."

Trump whinnied.

"Valet parking. Very nice. That will be fine, thank you. But how do you know why I'm here? I didn't get a chance to—"

"You're the forty-seventh prince to call on Princess Asnora this year, Your Majesty. I hope you don't mind that I made an assumption."

"Princess…Asnora…" Jack scratched his neck absently. He spun around to take in the view of the front entry way. Very grand. Very ornate. Very polished despite the inaccessibility of the various objects to any human polisher. "Nice place you have here. Either your cleaning staff can fly, or you've magically banished dust."

Without looking upward at the gleaming gargoyles, the butler droned, "Yes."

Jack blinked. "Yes, flying staff, or—?"

"Two flights up, four doors down to your right." The butler departed, his upper body motionless while his spindly legs folded and flapped in a silent display of gracelessness.

Jack found the room in question despite the lack of an escort. The entire castle seemed bereft of life, yet impeccably clean. Glancing down at his attire, he smiled with satisfaction at the anti-grime-and-dishevelment suit his mother had bought him. A lazy luxury, yes, but even hard workers hate doing laundry. It never ends, after all.

A young woman sat dutifully outside the door, perched on a stool in such a way that Jack suspected the voluminous folds of her dress hid core muscles of steel. As he approached, she jumped off and drew in a breath, extending her stature to its full capacity (which was not very capacious). "How may I help you, sir?" Something in her eyes implored him sincerely, as if this was not a courtesy request.

"I…" He paused, watching her bounce ever so slightly on her heels. "Are you all right, miss?"

"Yes, sir. Just eager to help, sir. Anything at all." She spoke rapidly and moved energetically, as if she had breakfasted on a Triple Grande Double Dutch Chocolate with Extra Cream and Two Pumps of Sugar with a Cinnamon Twist cup of over-priced coffee.

"Well, I understand there's a Princess…"

"Asnora, yes. Have you come to kiss her?"

"I…what?" Jack had taken Charming classes and was certain that Princess-kissing etiquette required at least one waltz before lips could be locked in any kind of nuptially binding way.

Instead of answering, the maid pushed open the door. "Follow me. I'll make sure she's ready."

"No guards to announce? Don't you want to know who I am?"

The young woman waved away his concern with a breezy laugh and led him to a latticed screen. "Wait here." She continued beyond, talking as she went. "If Butler let you in, you must be a prince, so there's always a chance, isn't there?"

"Butler. Yes."

"I'm just applying the lipstick," called the maid. "You can come back now."

"Oh, I—"

"She won't mind. Do you need a breath mint?"

Jack's brow knit so tightly that he couldn't see for a moment. "I'm sorry, what are you talking about?" He peeked around the screen expecting to see some kind of reception room, or throne room, or tea party, or anything but the huge, four-post bed draped with lacy gauze. His mouth flopped open in a stupor.

"I'll take that as a yes," chirped the maid, popping something into his mouth and lifting his chin back into position. She beamed up at him. "Go ahead as soon as it dissolves. She's quite ready."

Jack looked at the bed, squinting to make sure he wasn't imagining things. He looked down at the maid, who again bounced on her heels with gleeful suppressed excitement. He looked back at the bed and swallowed the mint whole. There was definitely someone lying on the bed. A girl-shaped someone. A very still, girl-shaped someone.

He looked back at the maid. "Look, Miss…"

"Espressa." Her eyes shone.

"Right. Miss Espressa, is it just me, or is she—?"

"Very beautiful. Oh yes, that's what they all say!"

"I was going to say 'asleep', actually."

"Well, of course she is!" Espressa flicked away an invisible fleck of dust from his shoulder. "Are you ready?"

"Either the customs in this kingdom are very different, or you were promoted to maid-in-waiting prematurely. This seems like a terrible breach of protocol…"

Espressa let out a giggle like sunshine. "I'm not a maid-in-waiting! The maids-in-waiting couldn't wait any longer. They all got married and have families of their own. Two of them are grandmothers now."

Jack leaned against the screen, very nearly toppling it. "I must be dreaming. None of this makes sense."

Espressa tugged at his wrist, her soft little hands strong despite their size. "Well that's just the point, isn't it? You're going to wake her from her dream."

"I wouldn't dare. Most people I know are terribly irritable when woken from a..." He consulted the grandfather clock on the wall. "Late morning nap."

"She won't mind," insisted Espressa. "Go ahead. Kiss her."

"But she doesn't even know me. I don't even know her."

Espressa tilted her head and rested her fists on her tiny waist. "Do you know all the people you're connected to on social media?"

"Well, I..."

"Kiss her already so I can move on from this guarding gig to something with some action!" This last bit came out with an alarmingly shrill tone which instantly evaporated into a petulant pout.

Jack raised a finger to begin a rebuttal, but thought better of it. "Right. Kiss Asnora." He shook his head. "Asnora? Really? Didn't her mother like her? That's a terrible name."

"It's my understanding that she was a very

sleepy baby." Espressa gestured fondly at the princess. "I suppose all that beauty rest paid off."

Jack gently pulled aside the gauze and took a good look at the Princess Asnora, snug in her bed, lovely and fully primped by her doting maid-on-a-stool-guard person. "She *is* very beautiful."

Espressa clapped her hands in a little flutter. "Go on. Kiss her."

"Well, I suppose that would wake her up." Shrugging, he leaned over and placed a polite kiss on her forehead.

"No, no, no! Not like that. Kiss her properly. On the lips. Why do you think I put on the lipstick?"

Jack was still staring at the princess, bewildered that she had not yet moved with all the talking and movement around her. "Are you sure?"

"Give her a good, *big* kiss!"

Not enjoying this quest as much as he would have imagined, Jack tried harder. He kissed the Princess Asnora on the lips and then took a step back.

"Wait for it." Espressa clawed at the air as if trying to pull the princess out of slumber. Gritting her teeth, she muttered, "Come on … Wake up …"

"Wow, she's a really sound sleeper." Jack shook his head. "I'll give it one more try, and then I probably need to move on." He knelt beside Princess Asnora, brushed a strand of her hair from her cheek and planted a movie-style kiss on her lips.

Nothing.

"Well, that was a singular waste of time." Espressa's whole body sagged with disappointment. "I really thought you might be the one."

Prince Jack stood up, frowning. "I didn't realize I was that bad at kissing."

"You looked like you were doing it right from where I was standing."

He shuffled uncomfortably away from Asnora. "It's kind of hard to get into it when she doesn't kiss back, you know."

Espressa nodded sympathetically. "I'm sure you meant well."

Jack scowled a little. "I'm pretty sure my kissing isn't that boring. I've never had anyone complain before."

"Of course not. Don't feel bad. It happens all the time."

"Not to *me*, it doesn't!" Jack impulsively took Espressa into his arms and gave her a passionate kiss, which she kindly reciprocated, thus re-establishing in his mind his capacity to smooch effectively. He let go of her, feeling flushed.

"Wow!" she swooned, and promptly passed out.

"You might try the Princess Peablossom, just three hills over," said Butler. "I understand she never sleeps at all."

Jack shrugged from atop Trump. "Well, that'll be fine as long as she doesn't talk every hour she's awake or insist on playing Candy Crush the whole time."

"I wouldn't know, sir." The butler bowed graciously and firmly closed the door behind him.

"Lead on, Trump. I forgot to ask which hills, so, you know, sniff her out, or something?"

Trump snorted, but took to a steady trot heading roughly eastward towards a wooded slope.

"Wake me when we get there, hey buddy? All that kissing wore me out."

Trump was careful to steer clear of the low-lying branches lest his master be unseated in his slumber, but when a gaggle of man-eating spiky bindles crowded the path, he took off at a full gallop.

Jack awoke to a smack on the cheek by a wayward twig and managed to lean forward into the saddle, grasping the reins for dear life as Trump showed off his signature speed. Unfortunately, he also showed off his signature running pattern, looping them back around to the left in a quarter-mile turn until they came upon the spiky bindles anew.

"Trump, I swear you're trying to get me killed."

This time, the vicious creatures swarmed, taking to the air around Jack in a swirling snarl of fangs and pointy bits that showed a complete disregard for all respectable laws of physics.

Jack abandoned his decorum (and some of his hair) as he urged Trump straight forward with a sustained squeal and flailing limbs. By the time they broke clear of the tree line, only two spiky bindles remained attached—one to Trump's half-eaten tail, and the other to Jack's left boot. No amount of kicking loosed its grip, but when Trump swooshed his tail wildly around his flank, the spiky bindle munching there was thrown free. It knocked into Jack's foot, in turn dislodging the last attacker's teeth. Jack and Trump raced onward, now able to adapt the more classic Prince-on-Galloping-Steed pose, though some of the effect was lost in profile because both man and horse had lost a lot of hair. Jack smoothed his palm over a stubbly patch on the top of his head and pondered whether or not the Buff Guy Extra Body Shampoo had saved his life by giving his "locks a life of their own," as per the advertisement. Perhaps his hair had been a decoy for the fleshier bits of his being.

At last they slowed to a lazy trot and took stock of the damage. The saddlebags were gone, along with Trump's toupee, but the anti-grime-and-dishevelment suit had done its job. As long as no one noticed the bad hair…

Jack hung his head in despair. "What does a prince have but his smile and his hair to capture a fair maiden's heart?" He silently cursed the shallowness of women and wished they would appreciate his personality and sparkling sense of humor instead of his looks. Spurring his horse back up to a canter, he groaned. "Come on, Trump. Try not to do anything else stupid until *after* I find a princess to marry."

The young woman who answered the door would have been beautiful if the bags under her eyes weren't large enough for toting groceries. She peered into the night's darkness behind Jack and frowned. "If you're here at this hour, I can only assume you've come about the bed. This way."

She turned and began marching up a flight of marble stairs with palpable weariness.

Jack decided introductions could wait until the morning and gladly followed the maid up to the guest quarters. He couldn't bring himself to be offended by the lack of fanfare because it was very late, after all.

As they climbed another two switchbacks of steep steps, Jack studied the half-asleep woman in front of him. She was remarkably well-dressed for a servant and the entrepreneurial side of him quickly surmised that a kingdom that could afford to dress its night servants in such finery was worth pursuing as an ally. Yes, a matrimonial merger could be very profitable. Unless the princess—assuming there really *was* a princess—had a really terrible flaw, he had found his fiscal true love.

Hopefully she wouldn't notice the hair.

The woman stopped in front of a double

door and leaned into both sides, pushing them wide open to reveal a gloriously elegant bedroom. Every detail showed refinement of taste. Every detail except the actual bed.

The bed seemed out of place.

Jack supposed this was because it was at least forty feet tall and surrounded by elaborate scaffolding. Propped on various platforms were mattresses of varying thickness and hue.

"Well, come on. What are you waiting for?" The woman to one of the ladders and started to climb.

Impressed by her stamina but confused by her intent, Jack just stared. "Ummm...."

The woman reached a platform and slumped onto it, her eyes barely open. "Are you going to help me, or not?"

"Help you what, miss? I'm afraid I don't understand."

She closed her eyes, but Jack could tell she was rolling them, too. He looked at the floor sheepishly and raked his remaining hair over the missing patch. "Too bad the spiky bindles ate the mane toupee," he thought.

"You aren't here to help me get more mattresses on top?" She yawned.

"I don't think so." He shook his head. "Perhaps I've come to the wrong palace?"

The woman rubbed the bridge of her nose and yawned again. "It is so hard to find good help nowadays. Where did you think you were going?"

Suddenly self-conscious, Jack decided cranking up his charming grin was his only chance. "I've come to seek the hand of the fair princess who dwells here."

The woman blinked at him very slowly. "Isn't that ironic? And all *she* wants is a *hand* getting a few more mattresses on the bed."

Jack's smile faltered. "Wait...what?"

Resuming her climb with an indignant sniff, the woman mumbled, "Lumpiest bed on the planet. Feels like I'm sleeping on boulders and broomsticks."

"*You're* the princess?"

"Princess Peablossom." She hefted up one corner of a mattress. "Do you have a name, or should I just call you Mr. Useless Scrufflenoggin?"

The princess! And she'd noticed the hair! "I'm sorry. I must have the wrong castle."

He backed out of the room, but not before he heard her grumble, "Stupid pizza delivery boys. Why don't they use a GPS on their bridles? Dumb fool probably got lost in the spiky bindle forest."

Jack stepped outside and into a fresh pile of horse droppings. The boot which had been punctured by the spiky bindle did not resist the ooze.

Staring at his steed, Jack growled, "Valet parking or no, it is not polite to poop on princesses' porches. Everyone knows that."

Trifecta Trumper snorted and plodded off, his nose high in the air.

Jack looked at him. "Trump, you're fired!"

Jack made it home on foot two weeks later, having enjoyed the solitary exertion. Of course, he avoided the spiky bindle forest on his route, but managed to make a bow and arrow and fell a momphibrak buck. The local village roasted it for him and sent him home with left-overs in a Tupperware satchel.

His mother kissed him on the cheek. "Welcome home, dear. Happy hunting?"

"In a manner, yes."

"Find a wife?"

"Not one that could stay awake."

"I'm sorry, dear." The queen frowned sympathetically. "Perhaps it isn't too late to take up an idle lifestyle? Then perhaps it wouldn't bother you so much if you had a sleepy bride?"

From the desk by the window, the king pointed eagerly at the computer screen. "Wait, Jack! Here's one! It was a recurring tweet, so I've ignored it until now, but it looks like there's a Princess Asnora that's been available for…seventy-two years now. All right, so there's a bit of an age gap there, but she's full heir to the throne now that everyone else in her family died…"

Jack shook his head. "I think I'll pass on that one, Dad."

The king sighed. "Very well. Make yourself useful and go interview the girl waiting in the hall. She wants a job, but I don't know where to put her to work."

"There's a girl in the hall?" He poked his head out of the room to see a familiar figure perched atop a stool, bouncing ever so slightly on her seat.

"Espressa!"

"Oh, is this *your* castle?" She sprang to the ground with even more energy.

"Yes, but whatever are you doing here?"

"I quit my job."

"What? Why? Were they mean to you?"

"What do you mean 'they'? It was just the butler and me, and I'm pretty sure he can handle the job of guarding the princess while she sleeps."

"Right."

She blushed. "I really thought you might be the one."

Jack beamed at her and took her hand. "I'm quite sure *you're* the one."

"You have work for me?"

"We can find a reason for you to stay," he said with a flirtatious lilt. "What are your specialties besides guarding sleeping princesses?"

"I could start by fixing your hair. Looks like spiky bindle spit there by your ear. Been there, done that. No worries." She pulled a pair of scissors from her apron pocket. "I'll have you looking dashing again in no time."

"Dashing? Again?" Jack's heart leapt and skipped and generally misbehaved. "Was I dashing the first time? I thought I put you to sleep."

Espressa giggled. "Don't let go this time, and I won't fall down when my knees go weak."

"I'll be sure to hold on tight." Fortunately, his Charming training kicked in, and he managed to maneuver her into his arms without seeming the least bit forward about it. While he kissed her most invigoratingly, she trimmed his hair to perfection with her eyes closed. (Her capacity to multi-task had been disgracefully underused in her last assignment.)

They were married the next day and lived happily, charmingly, and actively ever after.

STORMY JANE & THE DAMSEL IN DISTRESS

Stormy Jane grew up with an unusual exposure to fearsome things. Her father was a blacksmith whose fiery furnace belched flames and smoke all day. The sound of clanging metal was her constant companion. At night, the raging storms over the lake soothed her to sleep. Thunder was her lullaby, and lightning was her security lamp.

And, of course, there was her sole playmate—the serpent of the lake. (*Not* a sea serpent. Salt dries her scales.) She was ninety feet long and had sharp fins the size of courtly banners. Her mouth could hold a small platoon of full-grown men, and in fact, Jane often rode upon her lower teeth, grasping her fangs for balance while they whirled around the lake at great speeds. The serpent taught Jane to dive and swim and chew rocks. She taught Jane to shriek and leap and shimmy between the raindrops. Jane tried very hard to teach the lake serpent to floss and use sugar-free mints, but lake serpents don't put much stock in oral hygiene.

Despite her friend's terribly bad breath, only one thing really made Stormy Jane unhappy. She longed for a horse. She had seen knights riding out to her father's workshop to commission great works of steel and silver. She admired the armor and the flashing swords her father made for them, but mostly she wished she could have a horse of her very own. Alas, she was only a blacksmith's daughter living in a kingdom where only royalty could own a steed.

"Why in water would you want one of those scrawny little things?" asked the serpent. "You can ride with me any time you want."

Jane, careful not to offend her best friend, replied, "I suppose for those days when I wish to be a little less wet."

The serpent harrumphed. She had been growing more irritable of late. "When are you ever not wet? It hasn't stopped raining over this lake in twenty-seven years."

Stormy Jane surveyed the sky as it rumbled with thunder. "Yes, well. I've heard of something called a sunlight, and I thought I might go exploring one day, just, you know, to see if I could find one."

"Hmm," conceded the serpent. "That

might be interesting. But why the horse? Couldn't you just walk?"

Jane shrugged. "All the knights I've ever met ride horses when they go off on expeditions. I believe that's the expectation."

"Have you applied for a horse at the DMV?" asked the serpent.

"The Department of Majestic Vocations? No. I'm not a majesty."

The serpent clucked her long tongue and winced at something. "I'm pretty sure there are waivers you can get for heroic types born out of the castle."

Jane considered this. "It's worth a trip, I suppose."

"C'mon, there's a local lake branch. I'll take you!"

With Jane clutching tightly to her neck, the serpent dove deep into the lake—so deep that Jane became alarmed. She had never been to this particular underwater trench, though they had often darted over it in play. Just when she thought her lungs might implode (or explode—she wasn't sure which), the serpent slithered into an underwater cavern and then shot upwards, bursting to the surface with a triumphant leap.

Not far away, Stormy Jane saw a tiny, bureaucratic building with beige blinds. She swam ashore, heaved open the door, and entered a stale lobby with hard plastic seats and bad lighting.

"Take a number!" barked a voice from behind a tall counter in front of her.

"Um, actually I just have a quick question—"

"Take a number!"

Jane stood on tip-toe, trying to find the source of the voice. "But… there's no one else here."

"DMV procedure. If you want a Majestic Vocation, you take a number."

Rolling her eyes, Jane looked around the empty lobby for the numbered ticket dispenser. Her shoes squeaked loudly as she sloshed across the tile floor, but something told her no one would be putting up a yellow "Caution" sign any time soon.

She ripped the paper ticket from the dispenser. *364*.

"364? Really? Is that like since ever? How many customers could you possibly get down here, anyway?"

She approached the counter, but before she could try another peek, the voice boomed, "Now serving number 311."

"What? Are you kidding me? There are not 53 people ahead of me!"

A scaly, fish-eyed face loomed up over the counter for the first time and frowned at Jane. "Look, miss. You're going to have to wait your turn like everyone else. Take a seat."

"But there's—"

"Please try not to drip on the floor."

"The office is at the bottom of a lake!"

"Take a seat!"

Stormy Jane folded her arms and slouched to the floor on the spot. She spent the next fifteen minutes squeezing the excess water out of her hair before the fish face spoke again. "Number 325."

No one had yet entered the room, but at least the line was moving faster than she had anticipated. At this rate, she'd be out in an hour.

Forty-seven minutes later, the dripping puddle on the floor had tortured her long enough and she had to get up to go to the bathroom. It was out of toilet paper, but the air dryer worked exceptionally well. With a little of the old soap acting as mousse, she was able to style her hair quite fashionably before strolling back out into the lobby and slipping flat on her back in the wet trail she had left behind.

"Number 413!" called the worker.

"What?! That's not possible!" Stormy Jane

bounded over to the counter and heaved herself up where she could stare down at the little man behind it. "I've been waiting over an hour. There is no way you just went through 50 more people in two minutes!"

"You'll have to take another number."

Jane grasped his throat. Placing her paper ticket on his protruding tongue, she dropped him back in his seat. "*You* take a number!"

He sputtered angrily, but removed the ticket and sneered at it. The ink had gone all blurry. "Oh look. 413. You're next. Have you filled out all the necessary paperwork?"

Jane's coiffed hair wilted. "What?! What paperwork?"

"Aren't you applying for a Majestic Vocation?"

"Well, I came to find out if I even can. I'm not a princess or anything, but all I want is a horse, not a castle or anything."

"In that case, you'll need the EFP 25 form with a completed DIDRV."

"Look, little man. I don't speak Acronym. I just want a horse. You know, to go for a ride to some new places. Maybe find a sunlight or two?"

For a moment the man's fish-eyes glazed over. "A sunlight? I saw one of those once…" Then he slipped a clipboard onto the counter.

"Fill these out and return them no later than the 24th of the month. Have a nice day."

Before Jane could object, he placed a placard on the counter and walked away. *Out to lunch. Come back tomorrow.*

Jane stared at the forms. "How am I supposed to get these home dry in order to fill them out when the office is in an underwater cavern?!" she shouted after the man.

No answer.

Jane trudged drearily out the door and plodded back across the parking lot.

"So, how'd it go?" asked the serpent. "Took you long enough. Your hair looks nice like that. Dry. Different, but it works on you."

"Don't start with me." Jane explained the form predicament and concluded that riding a horse was more trouble than it was worth.

"Oh, there now," said the serpent. "You can store the papers in my mouth. Slide them between my teeth so they don't touch my tongue, and I'll keep my mouth shut while we swim home. Deal?"

"You're the best."

"That's why we're BFFs," agreed the serpent.

Back on the shore near her home, Stormy

Jane retrieved her paperwork. "Y'know, you really need to floss, girl. This clipboard isn't the biggest thing stuck between your teeth."

"Yeah, yeah. Nag, nag. Go inside and read where it's dry and let me know if there's anything I can do to help."

Jane waved good-bye and ran through the rain to her home while the lake serpent moaned and groaned about something Jane couldn't quite hear.

The next day, Jane arrived early enough at the DMV so that her wait was only an hour and a half. She slapped the clipboard down triumphantly. "There. The EFP 25— Exception for Peasants under 25 is all filled out. I've got my supplies gathered as per the instructions on page 13. By the way, what's with the 'hunk of cheese and half loaf of day-old bread' bit? We have a gourmet kitchen. Is there a law against packing some dried cranberry trail mix or a—"

"DMV procedure, miss. Do you have the DIDRV filled out?"

"Ah. Yeah. About that. Damsel in Distress Rescue Verification. Okay, so I'm thinking that's a little weird given that I am kind of in the damsel category myself."

The fish-eyed man failed to blink. "Yes, I suppose you are."

"So…" Jane gesticulated to show the giant wheels of logic that should be turning in his head. "Could we switch that requirement out to a dude in distress or something?"

"I don't understand."

"Could I rescue a boy?"

The man's non-existent eyebrows shot up. "Now there's an idea! Let me check." He tapped at his keyboard and frowned for several minutes. "Nope. Sorry. The fine print does specify that all MVs must be granted only to EFPs who save a person of the female—and unattached, as in single—persuasion."

Jane pouted. "That does seem a bit outdated, doesn't it?"

"I wasn't working here when they wrote it."

"Can't you change it?"

"No, sorry. You're going to have to find a female damsel type in distress and fix the situation. If she can give you some kind of token of her gratitude or proof of your rescuing venture, you bring that back and voila, you can get your horse permit."

"Does that come with a horse?"

"If that's what you really want."

"Yes."

"Not very ambitious, are you? Most knights want the horse in order to go on a quest to win a princess and a new kingdom."

"I don't need a princess. I need a horse."

"You could probably be granted an honorary princess-ship." He started to write something on her form, but Stormy Jane snatched it away.

"Just the horse."

"I'll still need the completed DIDRV."

Jane banged her forehead on the counter three times. "Where am I supposed to find a damsel in distress?" Her jaw hurt from clenching it so tightly.

"Most of the knights say riding out to the eastern kingdoms is usually—"

"If I had something to *ride*, I wouldn't be here in the first place!"

"I'm sorry, miss. DMV procedure is—"

Jane's frustrated scream echoed through the lobby.

The serpent's scream echoed across the lake.

"Wow, what is your problem today?" asked Jane.

"My whole mouth hurts. Are you sure you

didn't leave another clipboard, or maybe a stapler in there?"

Jane climbed into the serpent's mouth and studied the teeth. "Your gums are pretty puffy. I told you to—"

"RAAAUURRGGHHWWWAAAA!!!"

Jane poked the inside of the serpent's cheek. "That was totally uncalled for. I'm trying to help. Quit being such a baby. Now let me get some rope and I'll get all this junk out from your mouth."

For the next two hours, Jane did battle with the lake serpent's gingivitis inflamed gums, picking and prying out fish bones, anchors, and abandoned paddleboat parts. And all through it, the serpent rasped and screeched, howled and writhed her neck in a flailing tantrum. Jane held on to a bicuspid and worked to alleviate her friend's oral discomfort.

"Fair maiden!"

Jane and the serpent stopped, confused, and looked around the rainy shoreline.

"Did you hear a man's voice?" asked Jane.

The voice came again. "Young damsel! Are you in distress?"

"I hink ere's a guy o'er 'ere," said the serpent, trying hard not to squish Jane in her mouth.

"Oh, yes. Over there."

"Fair damsel! Are you in distress?" called the man a little too eagerly.

"Um, no?" She studied him. "He must be a knight," she mumbled. "Very handsome. Nice horse."

"Is that foul serpent trying to eat you?" he called.

"Nope, she's just in a lot of pai—wait a minute!" shouted Jane crossly. "You get your own damsel in distress to rescue!"

"What?"

"Back off, buddy. This is *my* damsel in distress! *I'm* rescuing her!"

"I beg your pardon?"

Jane shook her head and muttered. "He's not the brightest, is he?"

The serpent tried to respond, but she couldn't speak clearly with all the things sticking out of her mouth. Jane grabbed onto a fang and swung down so she dangled below the serpent's maw.

"Wanna run that by me again, friend?"

"Not smart," said the serpent. "But he's got a horse. Maybe you two could work something out?"

Jane looked up at her friend and smiled. "You are a genius! Now rinse and spit." She dove into the water. "I gotta go see a man about a horse."

Before she could haul herself from the water, the knight trotted up to her (the horse waited further back) and swept Jane into his arms. "Sweet damsel! Let me take you from this dismal place!"

"Um, no thanks. But I've got a proposal for you."

Startled, the knight all but dropped her. "I believe that's my job."

"Not a marriage proposal, silly!"

"I hate to sound shallow," said the knight. "I mean, you're very beautiful and all, but how big is your father's kingdom?"

Stormy Jane gave him a look that would have started a thunderstorm if there hadn't already been one raging. She wriggled free and stood with hands on her hips. "No marriage. I only want one thing." She pointed. "That horse."

He smiled benignly. "Of course we shall ride away on the horse and live happily ever after … pending the size of your father's kingdom."

"No, no. *I* shall ride away on the horse. You shall go file my paperwork for me in the DMV that makes it legal for me to own a horse."

"Wait, you're not a princess?"

"Nope. Just a dismal damsel. Look, if you need a selfie of you battling a dragon or something fierce, my friend can probably help you out. Just keep it blurry."

The knight's eyes shone with relief. "Really? I needed a POHA form!"

Stormy Jane stared at him.

"Proof of Heroic Act. Most of the five-star kingdoms demand that on your resume anymore."

"Oh. Right. Go for it. Now gimme your horse."

The knight, though thoroughly bewildered by all he had seen, was more than happy to exchange his horse for Jane's DIDRV form and a few pictures of him "battling" the lake serpent. So while he swam to the underwater cavern and waited in line for nine hours, Stormy Jane rode away on her new trusty steed in search of a sunlight.

She found one at the top of a nearby hill, once she had cleared the rain clouds. It was nice, but overrated. She ended up letting the horse go free on a grassy meadow and trudged her way home to her father and her best friend.

Three weeks later, she received a package

in the mail. She sat with the serpent on the shore while she opened it.

"Oh look," said the serpent. "An honorary princess crown!"

Stormy Jane smirked. "Wheee." She stuffed it between the serpent's molars. "Let's go for a swim!"

While on a nice, deep dive, they heard a voice call, "Now serving number 622."

ABOUT THE AUTHOR

Lia London started out writing in her childhood, focusing on writing comic sketches for school assemblies and camps. After a few decades of that, she graduated up to writing longer works, including many novels available through Amazon or Barnes & Noble. She lives with her husband, two teens, and two silly pets in Oregon, USA. She loves reading, watching the funny sketch show "Studio C", and taking water aerobics ~ which is a comedy routine in itself.

Longer works of humor by Lia London include a romantic comedy called *Her Imaginary Husband* and a cozy mystery called *The Fargenstropple Case*.

Made in the USA
Charleston, SC
13 November 2016